THE SPHERE

N. A. GAD

A Paradigm

The Sphere

Written by Nicolaas A Gad

Copyright © 2025 by Nicolaas A Gad

Self-Published by

Nicolaas A Gad

albertgad67@gmail.com

ISBN: 978-1-7637114-3-3

First Edition: July, 2025

Cover Design by Nicolaas A Gad

Printed in Australia

INDEX

I seem to be in the presence of a self transforming sphere of colour, sound, and all things, that appears in front of me but fully encapsulates me to the point where I forget I am merely interacting with it.

And as I interact with it, I realise that for every one of my actions, it will react accordingly.

I find that what I expect in reality is reflected in my actions towards it, and so it reveals that part of itself to me.

If I expect a positive world, I myself become positive, and reality reveals its positive features.

If I expect a negative world, I find I am negative towards it, and so it responds negatively in return.

If I expect a task will be easy, I will approach it in a way that is simpler and more holistic, and so the task will seem easier.

If I expect to be judged negatively, I behave insecurely, and so open myself up to negative judgment.

My interaction with this thing is as if I am in the presence of another entity, that responds accordingly to my every output.

And during my interaction with this entity, there is an innate desire within me to do better; to move my life from negative to positive. It is a gravitation towards wanting to be good, and wanting things to be good, and so I unconsciously work towards attaining goodness.

And at the ultimate end of the spectrum - at the pinnacle of the gradient - is goodness itself; a perfect form of a positive nature. Some tell me this is what God is.

However I find it difficult to reconcile the fact that God is described as all encompassing, however does not encompass what is negative. How can a single God that is all there is, be defined only as all that is good.

That is, unless, what I define as bad is just a lack of good. Perhaps there is no negative, and just an absence of positive, as cold is the absence of heat, or as dark is the absence of light.

In this way, light and dark is comparable to something and nothing, and so is good and bad. And so in our lives we see glimpses of nothingness remaining in a world of something. The something envelopes the nothingness, but not entirely, and so we see the darkness spawn where it can amongst the light that hasn't shone it out of existence.

And in this experience, I find I am on a journey, and I know that my journey is leading somewhere, however I never reach the destination in totality. I arrive to where I think I was headed, only to see the path extend in front of me. I am coming to understand that the destination I seek to rest at in life is the static state of being I have whilst within the journey. It is the maintenance of my way of being whilst travelling to where I am going that is the place I strive to arrive at. In this way, the journey is the destination. And so I continue in my journey towards seeking warmth, light and goodness.

1

As I continue in this journey and travel along the path set before me, I cannot stop my contemplation of the unnerving reality that I am.

In this world made of something, I appear, conscious and experiencing it. We are taught the world is made of matter - dead and unalive substances that somehow comprise to create an animated version of itself that we call life. I am such a thing; a perfectly formed character as if one that was creatively thought up.

It seems so perfect that we come from inanimate physical matter, to become fully formed characters that can interact with others, have personality, and make sense of ourselves and the world we find ourselves in.

It is so perfect that we can both exist in the world and make sense of it - that the world we find ourselves in allows for us to exist within it, and to be able to perceive it and experience it. It is so perfect to be made out of it, and be able to have a perception of it. I see how fortunate it is that the mind can understand itself, and that the universe can experience itself.

It is also so perfect to be constructed in such complex ways at the micro scale, but at a large scale seem so simply drawn and moulded. We are constructions of the smallest substances with such detail that when perceived from afar blend to create an animated artwork. Somehow the complex detail of the minute merges to become holistic and simple again when looked at as one. It seems there is an intelligence in this.

And it is not only us, but all plants and animals too have their own perfectly understandable characters. It is as if life is the imagined manifesting in the physical. The physical matter we often pass off as very real and unmagical animates itself to represent that which is imagined and not physical - and further, this animated matter serves as a gateway to manifest more imagined ideas into physical form, as humans create.

And so what we see becomes both at the same time, physical and imagined. A merging of what we understand to be separate to become one.

And while this concept and others can give new and exciting perspectives on life, they do not teach how to live it. I can conceptualise and reform my idea of what this life and existence is in infinite ways that, when believed, becomes true to me. Sometimes these paradigms can provide a new way to approach life, and a new outlook that affects my behaviour either positively or negatively, but regardless of which view on life I have, and which paradigm I exist within, I find it doesn't affect what lessons arise.

Something common to all the perspectives of life that I have embodied are that I am being taught. I experience lessons that are taught to me by the world. These are taught, learned, retaught and relearned until they become part of the practice of how I live.

The idea of what the world is to me doesn't make a difference to what the world teaches me. Whether the world is a dream, a physical one, one created by God or one Godless - in each, the same process is present of me being a student, and the universe being a teacher.

And if I don't wish to be the student, and I ignore the lessons I should be learning, I find each lesson is taught to me again until I learn what needs to be learned. I repeat what has happened before in new ways, and encounter similar themes and patterns until I can break free by understanding what reality is telling me, and practicing this new found knowledge accordingly.

2

As I pay attention to my experience, and become conscious of the fact that I am being taught, I question who I am being taught by. I find I am interacting with something. This student-teacher relationship is one way I interact with this thing, but I also interact with it in many other ways. It is a relationship I develop, however it is not immediately obvious who or what this relationship is with.

I peer into the space in front of me, and at first I see many things, all separated by the labels I attach to them. I don't notice that my field of experience is one field; an energy I am in the presence of, beautifully illustrating an existence that so elegantly combines everything in a way that makes sense to me and becomes cohesive.

When I look at everything as one, I find what I am interacting with; a sphere of energy that presents itself to me as colours, sounds, feelings, and all things.

As the sphere and I interact, I find it is leading me somewhere. I follow the path it sets before me, led by a feeling that there is meaning to be found along the way. It gives me purpose to follow it, to learn what it is teaching, to enjoy what it is showing. It feels right to go in the direction it points, and I no longer feel alone as I once did.

I am no longer wandering aimlessly and struggling to create direction by myself. Tasks are no longer tasks but scenery along my walk. Things are easier because they are a natural part of the journey, provided by something else, rather than forced actions I impose on myself.

As I follow this path, opportunities arise and events occur, and I am learning that I should choose to follow them, remembering I am being led.

I am tempted to resist, and to say no when offered a new direction. Part of me wants to remain comfortable and for things to remain predictable, but I know that the magic fades when I sit still. I know that I should take the hand that is leading me when it presents itself.

The path is not all beautiful, though, as I sometimes wish it was. I cannot expect to grow without resistance. I know I cannot expect to learn patience without having to wait, or to learn courage without treacherous times. And so I sometimes find myself in parts of this path that are dark and desolate. Sometimes I wander from green and open fields into lightless tunnels, and when I realise where I am, my instinct is to resist.

I am tempted to turn back, or to walk more slowly and carefully, resisting moving forward as all I can see ahead is more discomfort. I can't be sure if this cave leads back to the surface, and I tend to imagine it continues deeper to a place that I cannot escape. I feel as though I may be buried here, but I have to trust that I will find a way out.

And that way out is always through. As the passing of time pushes me forward, I know I cannot come out the same way I entered. I cannot turn back and change my decision to enter the cave, and I know resistance will only prolong my visit to the darkness. I have to trust that the hand that led me in here will also lead me out; but I must be willing to embody what I have learned in the cave to find the exit.

So I continue forwards, feeling into the darkness and accepting and admiring this part of the journey for what it is. I am not just trying to pass through, but to learn what I need to while I am here. I have to develop a trust for the process to maintain my steady pace. Eventually, the light appears ahead, and so I follow it out.

And as I am engulfed in light, and the weight on my mind releases, I realise the darkness was made of thoughts, and only when I developed enough to change my thoughts did I realise the weight I carried was internal. My own mind blanketed my present moment with chaos - a turbulent mind cast me in the shadow of the light that was all around, but I could not see out as it entirely occupied my mental space.

Through attention to the lessons being presented to me, I could align my internal state accordingly to let the light in again. I must remember that hard times are not punishment, but a time to be taught by the teacher, who never left my side. I was never alone in the darkness, and the teacher's presence was always there, I just needed to acknowledge its company and notice what the teacher was teaching.

Now that I am free from the darkness, the light seems lighter than it was before. I can now appreciate the openness and freedom more fully than prior to being trapped. And so again, I have been taught by the teacher, and have emerged with a new perspective. The darkest paths can lead to the lightest light, only if we understand what each dark moment is for.

While keeping notes of its lessons, and trying not to forget, I am learning more about both myself and this energy that accompanies me.

It is not just my teacher, but also my friend. Whilst invisible within my life, it responds to my intentions and expectations. I must pay attention to notice how it responds, or things seem random and without meaning once again, but if I do pay close attention, I can hear it's rebuttal.

3

My expectations of reality, and my own outlook and output reflect back to me. If I am in a positive mood, and expect a positive day, the day is positive. I approach others positively, and so others respond to me positively.

If I am calm, and expect others to be calm, I find that I experience a day of peace. Reality seems to respond in like to how I treat it, and so I try to treat it nicely.

Sometimes when I am not focussed, or living without intention, I treat reality poorly. When I do this, it retaliates. When I treat the world without respect, I am not respected. When I am unhappy with the world, the world is unhappy with me. When I am not kind to the world, the world is not kind to me. The worlds negative response to my own negativity can further create more unhappiness in myself.

For example, when I am annoyed with reality, I am annoyed with people, and so people are annoyed with me. They treat me poorly, because I treat them poorly, and soon, all I see around me is mistreatment. This negativity depresses me and puts me in a worse mood than I was in before, and so I descend to further depths of a growing depression.

This cycle continues until I become aware of it and can break free, but sometimes it has been so long that it is hard to remember how to be positive again. I become accustomed to my way of being, and comfortable in knowing how things will continue. Changing now means things will be unpredictable once again, even if they are unpredictably better.

But I know that I cannot remain how I am. I cannot continue in predictable darkness, so I decide to change. I know that to be treated with love I must first treat others with love. And so to break free I must initiate what I wish to be reflected. In these moments, I cannot be the mirror, but must be the light.

If I am the mirror, and reality is also a mirror, the reflection of negativity will be eternal as it is caught between me and reality. I must first be the light, to have light reflected back, and once it is so, only then can I change to become the mirror.

This way, I trap light and positivity in eternal reflection. But I must know how to be the light in the darkest of times. I must know how to reshape judgment into admiration, jealousy into inspiration, dislike into love. I must instigate what I wish my world to be, as I know ultimately I am the cause of my own mental suffering.

I must befriend reality itself, and love reality itself, for it to love me back. I cannot expect too much of it if I do not expect anything of myself. I cannot expect it to teach me if I am not willing to learn. I know that reality will treat me well if I treat it well, and I understand that reality is raising me, but I must first be willing to rise.

I am grasping the relationship I have with this energy in new ways. We are coming to understand each other, and how to best interact. I understand my role, and am learning the role that it plays in my experience.

Because of this understanding, I maintain a level of respect for reality. I understand the power it has to encourage my growth, or to put me in my place.

4

The lessons never end, and there is no point of rest. I walk away from one only to reach the next. When I reach as far as I could see, the path extends before me. I thought the end was there, but I just could not see around the next corner.

There is always more path, even when it feels like I am not moving fast, or when the next steps seem uncertain. I realise generally it is the people around that offer those next opportunities and the next stone to step on.

If I open up and am receptive to what arises, I find the path is easier to see. I need not be so in control all the time. I need not get caught up in my own rigid plans. To break out of any meaningless lull I get myself into I need to open up to what is being offered.

Part of any lull arises from me being closed off, and part of it is my expectations of how things should be.

For example, I often find I am chasing happiness. I expect the path to always be pleasant. If I expect ecstasy, a high state of being, all of the time, this expectation always leaves me feeling like I am falling short of how I should feel. If I am not happy, then I must be sad. If everything is not always at the peak, I must be in the trough.

But I am learning what I should strive for instead is peace, and to find this, I can start with relinquishing what I cannot change.

There are things I can change, and that I do have control over, and for those things, I should spend energy on them. But for what I cannot change, energy spent here is energy wasted.

I have come to learn there are three parts to what I cannot change: what I can't change in the past, what I can't change in the present, and what I can't change in the future.

I have learned that there is no reward in the exercise of 'what if'. Reflecting on the past is a practice that can yield valuable lessons, however there is no fruit for me from wishing to change the past.

If things have already been, then that is how they were. It is impossible for my current self to make decisions for my past self, or my future self to make decisions for my current self. I should not want what is impossible, because that would leave me indefinitely in disappointment.

I must first accept things for how they are now, and then learn to appreciate and love things for how they are now. I can do this by understanding that how now is is how now should be.

I must understand that what I have been through was absolutely necessary to get me to where I am now.

I must understand that if things were different, there is no guarantee they would be better.

I must understand that each dark moment provided invaluable lessons that I would not have without them. For these moments, I should be grateful, as they are a gift. These moments provide true insight into what so few understand.

And so follows that I must understand that wisdom comes from true experience.

All experiences were necessary to create the person I am, and rejecting past experiences would be rejecting myself.

And so I understand reality has provided me my past to serve my present. I must trust in the process, and trust that what I have been taught was for a reason.

And as the future becomes the present, and the present becomes the past, what is true for the past is true for both others - the same applies. But the present and future are still malleable, and I understand for these there are diminishing, or even negative, returns in trying to perfect them. I understand to truly be satisfied I must relinquish absolute control, and take imperfection in my eyes as perfection in the eyes of reality. My ideal is not the ideal, and the ideal is what is.

5

In my journey, I encounter many others. I learn from them, find my path through them, and share reality with them. I must be aware though of the different people I encounter, as some detract from my journey, and take from me for themselves. Some do this intentionally, and others unintentionally, however the effect they both have are the same.

From these individuals I am provided many lessons, one of which is to not model my idea of goodness after those that I meet. Even if I perceive them as being good, I have learned that positively natured and wholly good are not the same.

I must find a consistent and reliable model of goodness to follow, that is firmly grounded and solid, and not malleable or determined by impermanent and changing things. And since the external world is ever changing, my model for goodness must be intrinsic and not sourced externally.

I must find this model for goodness as I understand that to receive goodness from reality I must project goodness into reality. To receive love I must project love. And this isn't just projecting the idea of good, or the idea of love, but projecting the thing itself.

I must strive to act wholly good to receive whole goodness. I must, with my actions, show love to all things, to be fully in the presence of love. And when I do so wholly and fully, I am accompanied by a wholly good and loving reality.

Without this attention to how I act and am, I find myself in a desolation. I find I am alone and without the company of the universe. This is unlike any cave I have been lead into to learn. This is an isolation and abandonment I feel in my whole body. Without my intention to do good, I become separate from the energy that I have come to know and love.

This is why I must focus not on my own hedonistic desires and persuit of self pleasure, but on what is in its nature unquestionably good. And what is good in itself is written into reality - it is not hard to discern what is good or bad, as we are innately provided with the guidance to determine this for ourselves. I find the model for goodness I must follow is within, and to sense it all I must do is listen to that inner guidance with close attention.

6

When I follow this goodness, and maintain a certain level of understanding for my experience, I feel an energy everywhere. I understand there are steps to perceiving the world for what it really is, and when I do, I feel a connection to everything.

Colours seem brighter, as I understand colours are not out there in the world, but are inside my experience, and so are a part of me. I can begin to see sounds, and experience them as a part of me also, as I understand they do not exist apart from inside my own experience of them. When I experience reality this way, everything becomes connected and a part of me.

My first step into seeing reality differently is to know that what exists in the world are waves - waves in the air that I interpret as sound, waves of light that I interpret as being different colours. But these sounds and colours are a subjective experience, and non physical. The sounds and colours are not the waves themselves, but represent the waves so I can distinguish them. The experience of these colours and sounds are called qualia. They exist in a place I cannot fully describe, that becomes more real than reality itself when I truly put my attention on them for what they really are.

When I delve deeper into perceiving colours as non physical, the world glows with beauty, as if illuminated by a different light than what the sun provides. Objects become electric, a hologram of my experience rather than a physical and separate thing from me. I understand that the world is imagined and created in my experience of it, and is not as physical, lonely or disconnected as other times it has felt.

I feel a oneness and connection with everything, and can feel reality around me as if it is a part of myself. It is as if I have access to a part of me I had forgotten how to feel.

I must pay close attention to maintain this experience of reality. I must maintain a goodness, and an understanding that what I see is I, and I am what I see. I must be able to look at a colour for what it really is, rather than be fooled by the illusion that it is somehow a physical thing. And it is just that thought, that colour cannot be physical, that can be the door to lead me to seeing reality for what it is.

This door leads me to realise that nothing is physical, and all of reality is made from ideas. I understand that reality is a construction of some sort of mental light, that portrays a physical reality, but is not a physical reality itself. This is in the same way that an image of something portrays what it is an image of, but is not the thing itself.

When I perceive the world in this way, my vision widens. It is as if I am looking at a screen, and can now see the pixels, rather than be fooled into thinking that what is on the display is what the display is constructed of.

If I examen the smallest parts of physical reality, down to cells and atoms, I do not get any closer to finding the base construct of reality, as the display I look through remains the same. I must examen and magnify the pixels of the monitor to see what reality is made from, not magnify and examen the world the monitor is portraying. The world the monitor portrays doesn't exist in the same way as the monitor does, as it is merely a representation of an idea.

And this display of reality is an energy of immense beauty, that we so often look through but not at. Until I train myself to see the screen, and not what is on the screen, I will always be fooled into seeing reality as physical.

7

From what I can observe, the display I look through appears to be a form of energy, expressing itself as a world that it can use to interact with me. And when I place my focus onto myself, at my core I am just an observer, and nothing more, enjoying the show and being provided an experience that I otherwise would not have.

And as I get immersed more deeply into this experience, I forget what I really am, and begin to identify with the character I play as. I begin to attach myself and be pulled into the story I am given.

And through this immersion I attain a sense of not knowing, and experience a forgetfulness as my memory of this world fills all of my awareness, and my awareness of what I truly am becomes lost behind it.

But when this facade fades for moments I remember that I am an observer, and I feel I am eternal. I am outside of the construct of time, and so exist for no time and forever at the same time. But when I am experiencing the sphere, and am immersed in experiencing a life, I am given the feeling of fleeting impermanence.

The character I play experiences change and so experiences time, while the pure awareness I am that witnesses life experiences no change, and so no time. It is as if while experiencing this energy, I have been placed on the tracks of procession, that gives me a sense of past and future, memories and hopes, provides me with a sense of ageing and traps me in an ongoing yet seemingly finite existence.

Things are fleeting and ever changing, and as I identify with the experience, I begin to believe this is all there is. The progression toward the end of the the tracks is like an unstoppable march toward the edge of a cliff, where something meets the abyss of nothing, and where I do not know what I will fall into.

But I don't realise in the moment that once I reach the edge and cross over into the openness on the other side, I will be stripped of my character, and I will once again identify with the awareness I have always truly been.

I realise that time is in a way an illusion. It does exist in terms of being a progression of events, but it is something provided by the display, and I am always in the present, and that does not change.

Whether outside or inside the experience of time, this sense of being remains, and being in one moment remains. And so wishing to be in one moment and not the next, or trying to escape the present moment by distracting myself, is a pointless endeavour, as this sense of being in the present is all that exists, and is inescapable.

It becomes an impulsive habit whilst existing to try to escape the deep awareness that I am. In this awareness at its core, I feel that I exist as an observer, and it is forever in the way that the things around me change but my awareness as an observer does not. I cannot escape the reality that I am always in the present, and that as the observer I am unchanging.

And so whether I am doing one activity or another, or looking forward to something more than I am appreciating the now, I must come to understand that being in the now is all there is, and so I should learn to enjoy it.

8

How easy it is to forget and not notice how incredibly lucky we are to be able to have an experience. To exist rather than to not exist, and that existence and the vividness of the experience is even possible.

To marvel at its complexity is one thing, but to marvel at its existence is another. The existence of existence is in itself a miracle. It is a magic that when we do not look at it but through it to see the world we do not see how unfathomably divine it is.

It is not only a perfectly functioning reality, but one that is also beautiful. It holds all that can be imagined within it, in some form or another. It is a perfectly balanced universal spectrum, where differentiation of one thing to another has allowed for all things to be. And in this balance, lies all from darkness itself to lightness itself.

And just as things inside the spectrum have identity, the entirety of it has an identity of itself. It is something that teaches, plays, cares for, enjoys, interacts with, and loves us. And while it can be easy to forget to see it for what it is as we experience it, it is always there as everything that we experience.

We are always accompanied by the teacher; this sphere that allows us to get lost within it, yet every so often reminds us to step back and say hello once again. And it is the relationship with it that can provide the most meaning.